Renewing

the Vision

A FRAMEWORK FOR CATHOLIC YOUTH MINISTRY

UNITED STATES CONFERENCE OF CATHOLIC BISHOPS • WASHINGTON, D.C.

In September 1976, the United States Catholic Conference's Department of Education issued *A Vision of Youth Ministry* with young people by blending the best of past efforts with emerging ideas from leaders across the country. Two decades later, the Church's ministry with adolescents is confronted by new challenges and opportunities. *Renewing the Vision: A Framework for Catholic Youth Ministry* is a blueprint for the continued development of effective ministry with young and older adolescents. After wide consultation with dioceses, national organizations, and youth ministers throughout the country, the Committee on the Laity submitted the final draft to the plenary assembly of the National Conference of Catholic Bishops. The document was approved on June 20, 1997, and is hereby authorized for publication by the undersigned.

Monsignor Dennis M. Schnurr
General Secretary
NCCB/USCC

First printing, August 1997
Sixth printing, February 2002

ISBN 1-57455-004-7

Contents

Introduction

Over the past two decades, the Church in the United States has been greatly enriched by the renewal of ministry with adolescents. In September 1976, the Department of Education of the United States Catholic Conference issued a new vision for ministry with young people that blended the best of past efforts with emerging ideas from leaders across the country. *A Vision of Youth Ministry* articulated the philosophy, goals, principles, and components of a new direction in the Church's ministry with adolescents. This vision was expressed as: "Youth Ministry is the response of the Christian community to the needs of young people, and the sharing of the unique gifts of youth with the larger community" (p. 6). This pattern of responding to the needs of young people and involving young people—with their gifts and energy—in the life of the community guided the dynamic approach to ministry presented in *A Vision of Youth Ministry*.

Renewing the Vision: A Framework for Catholic Youth Ministry builds on the fine tradition begun by the 1976 document, *A Vision of Youth Ministry*. It has been expanded to address the call to personal discipleship, evangelization, and leadership. To respond to the new challenges and opportunities of our day the Catholic bishops of the United States offer *Renewing the Vision*—a blueprint for the continued development of effective ministry with young and older adolescents.

Renewing the Vision is a call to make ministry with adolescents a concern for the entire church community, especially for leaders in parishes, schools, and dioceses. The Holy Father has emphasized repeatedly the importance of young people and ministry with them. His words at World Youth Day 1995 called the Church to become the "traveling companion of young people."

> What is needed today is a Church which knows how to respond to the expectations of young people. Jesus wants to enter into dialogue

with them and, through his body which is the Church, to propose the possibility of a choice which will require a commitment of their lives. As Jesus with the disciples of Emmaus, so the Church must become today the traveling companion of young people. . . . (*Youth: Sent to Proclaim True Liberation*, World Youth Day 1995, Philippines).

Renewing the Vision takes up the Holy Father's challenge by focusing the Church's ministry with adolescents on three essential goals: (1) empowering young people to live as disciples of Jesus Christ in our world today; (2) drawing young people to responsible participation in the life, mission, and work of the faith community; and (3) fostering the personal and spiritual growth of each young person. To accomplish these goals it will take the people and resources of the entire Church. *Renewing the Vision* offers a practical framework for utilizing the resources of the entire faith community *and* integrating ministry with adolescents and their families into the total life and mission of the Church.

Renewing the Vision is most importantly an affirmation of the faith, gifts, energy, and fresh ideas of young people. It is a Christ-centered vision. It is a call to empower young people for the mission they have been given by the Lord Jesus. As the Holy Father said to the young people gathered in Denver at World Youth Day 1993:

> At this stage of history, the liberating message of the Gospel of life has been put into your hands. And the mission of proclaiming it to the ends of the earth is now passing to your generation, the young Church. We pray with the whole Church that we can meet the challenge of providing "coming generations with reasons for living and hoping" *(Gaudium et Spes,* no. 31).

+ G. Patrick Ziemann

Most Reverend G. Patrick Ziemann
Committee on the Laity

+ Roger L. Schwietz

Most Reverend Roger L. Schwietz, OMI
Subcommittee on Youth

PART ONE

The Growth and Development of the Church's Ministry with Adolescents

Signs of Hope

One of the most hopeful signs over the past two decades in the Catholic Church in the United States has been the renewal of ministry with adolescents.

A Vision of Youth Ministry initiated a transformation in the Church's thinking and practice that has matured over the past two decades. It emphasized the following aspects of ministry with adolescents:

- **Ministerial and pastoral.** The pastoral, integrated vision of Church, expressed through the eight components (ministries of advocacy, catechesis, community life, evangelization, justice and service, leadership development, pastoral care, and prayer and worship) was grounded in a contemporary understanding of the mission and ministry of Jesus Christ and his Church. *A Vision of Youth Ministry* made it quite clear that ministry with young people was integral to the life of the Church. Far from peripheral to the Church's concern, ministry with adolescents was *essential* for helping the Church realize its mission with its young members.

- **Relational.** Effective ministry with adolescents was built on relationships. The central place of the Emmaus story in *A Vision of Youth Ministry* demonstrated the primacy of relationships and of discovering God within those relationships.

- **Goal-centered.** In articulating two primary goals for ministry, *A Vision of Youth Ministry* gave specific direction while encouraging leaders in local communities to create a variety of ways to reach their goals. There was no longer *one* way to minister to adolescents.

- **Multidimensional.** An effective ministry incorporated eight components with their program activities so that the needs of all the young people could be addressed and the resources of the community could be wisely used. This multidimensional approach was a needed response to social-only, athletics-only or religious education-only youth programming.

- **Holistic and developmental.** *A Vision of Youth Ministry* proposed an approach that attended to a wide spectrum of adolescent needs and that was attuned to the distinct developmental, social, cultural, and religious needs of adolescents.

- **People-centered and needs-focused.** *A Vision of Youth Ministry* focused on young people. It encouraged an approach designed to address the particular needs of young people in their communities. *A Vision of Youth Ministry* did not recommend program models or specific activities, recognizing that the day had passed when one program structure could respond to all the needs of youth.

A Vision of Youth Ministry was the catalyst for a dramatic increase in new and innovative pastoral practice with adolescents. Since the late 1970s, the Church has seen the growth of multidimensional parish youth ministries throughout the country, the emergence of the role of parish coordinators of youth ministry and Catholic high school campus ministers, the development and widespread availability of high quality youth ministry training programs and youth leadership training programs, an increase in the number of quality youth ministry resources, attention to the needs of families with adolescents, and expansion of the scope of ministry to include young and older adolescents.

We are very encouraged to see that the renewal of ministry with adolescents has had a positive impact on the lives of young people. The 1996 study of parish youth ministry program participants, *New Directions in Youth Ministry*, offers the first data on a national level specifically on Catholic youth ministry. The study is good news for the Church because it shows that adolescents who participate in parish youth ministry programs identify faith and moral formation as a significant contribution to their life, have a profound sense of commitment to the Catholic Church, attend Sunday Mass regularly, and show continued growth while they remain involved in youth programs. These are positive signs that the Church's investment in ministry with adolescents is making a difference in their lives and in the life of the Church.[1]

A New Moment

Two decades after the publication of *A Vision of Youth Ministry,* the Church's ministry with adolescents is confronted by three new challenges.

First, the changes in our society present the Church with a new set of issues. We are deeply concerned by America's neglect of young people. The United States is losing its way as a society by not ensuring that all youth move safely and successfully into adulthood. All across America, far too many young people are struggling to construct their lives without an adequate foundation upon which to build. We are also concerned about the consequences of the social and economic forces affecting today's families. The effects of consumerism and the entertainment media often encourage a culture of isolation. Far too many families lack sufficient time together and the resources to develop strong family relationships, to communicate life-giving values and a religious faith, to celebrate family rituals, to participate in family activities, and to contribute to the well-being of their community. Too many communities do not provide the economic, social service, and human development infrastructure necessary for promoting strong families and positive adolescent development.[2]

These new challenges can point to new opportunities for ministry. The Church's ministry with adolescents and their families has an important contribution to make in building healthy communities and in providing the developmental and relational foundation essential to a young person's healthy development. We need a vision and strategy that addresses these contemporary challenges.

Second, new research has provided insight into the factors that make for healthy adolescent development. Through its surveys with more than a quarter of a million adolescents in 450 communities across the United States, the Search Institute, a research organization dedicated to promoting the well-being and positive development of children and adolescents, has identified forty essential building blocks or assets for positive adolescent development, reflecting the extensive literature on child and adolescent development, resiliency, youth development, and substance abuse prevention. These forty building blocks[3] include *external assets* provided by the community through families, schools, churches, and organizations, and *internal assets* developed within the adolescent (e.g., commitment to learning, positive values, social skills, and positive identity). The Search Institute research on asset-building indicates that

- asset development begins at birth and needs to be sustained throughout childhood and adolescence;
- asset building depends on building positive relationships with children and adolescents, and requires a highly consistent community in which they are exposed to clear messages about what is important;
- families can and should be the most powerful generators of developmental assets;

- assets are more likely to blossom if they are nurtured simultaneously by families, schools, youth organizations, neighborhoods, religious institutions, health care providers, and in the informal settings in which adults and youth interact;
- everyone in a community has a role to play.

This model of healthy adolescent development offers practical direction for the Church's ministry today and in the future. Ministry with adolescents will need to be more comprehensive and community-wide to take full advantage of the opportunities presented by this research.

Third, the continuing development of the Church's understanding and practice of ministry since the publication of *A Vision of Youth Ministry* in the late 1970s needs to be incorporated into a contemporary vision and strategy for ministry with adolescents today. The following publications provide a foundation upon which to build this enriched and expanded vision and strategy: *The Challenge of Adolescent Catechesis: Maturing in Faith* (NFCYM, 1986), *The Challenge of Catholic Youth Evangelization: Called to Be Witnesses and Storytellers* (NFCYM, 1993), *A Family Perspective in Church and Society* (USCC, 1988), *Putting Children and Families First* (USCC, 1991), *Follow the Way of Love* (USCC, 1994), *Communities of Salt and Light* (USCC, 1993), and *A Message to Youth: Pathway to Hope* (USCC, 1995).

In order to respond to these challenges and opportunities, the Church's ministry with adolescents needs to enter a new stage in its development. *Renewing the Vision* is a blueprint for the continued development of effective ministry with young and older adolescents. Its expanded vision and strategy challenges leaders and their faith communities to address these challenges and to invest in young people today. We are confident that the Catholic community will respond by utilizing our considerable creativity, energy, and resources of ministry with adolescents. We are writing to inspire parish, school, and diocesan leaders to continue the fine tradition begun by *A Vision of Youth Ministry*—a tradition that continues to give birth to effective ministry with new generations of young people.

PART TWO

Goals for Ministry with Adolescents

As leaders in the field of the youth apostolate, your task will be to help your parishes, dioceses, associations, and movements to be truly open to the personal, social, and spiritual needs of young people. You will have to find ways of involving young people in projects and activities of formation, spirituality, and service, giving them responsibility for themselves and their work, and taking care to avoid isolating them and their apostolate from the rest of the ecclesial community. Young people need to be able to see the practical relevance of their efforts to meet the real needs of people, especially the poor and neglected. They should also be able to see that their apostolate belongs fully to the Church's mission in the world (cf. Pope John Paul II, *Listen to the True Word of Life*, 1993).

Three interdependent and equally important goals guide the Church's ministry with adolescents.[4] These goals state what it means for the Catholic community to *respond* to the needs of young people and to *involve* young people in sharing their unique gifts with the larger community. They express the Church's focus for ministry with adolescents, while encouraging local creativity in developing the programs, activities, and strategies to reach these goals.

Goal 1: To empower young people to live as disciples of Jesus Christ in our world today.

Ministry with adolescents helps young people learn what it means to follow Jesus Christ and to live as his disciples today, empowering them to serve others and to work toward a world built on the vision and values of the reign of God. As we wrote in *A Message to Youth*:

As a baptized member of the Church, Jesus Christ calls you to follow in his footsteps and make a difference in the world today. You *can* make a difference! . . . In the words of the Holy Father: "Offer your youthful energies and your talents to building a civilization of Christian love . . . commit yourself to the struggle for justice, solidarity, and peace" (*Homily at World Youth Day,* Denver, 1993).

The challenge of discipleship—of following Jesus—is at the heart of the Church's mission. *All ministry with adolescents must be directed toward presenting young people with the Good News of Jesus Christ and inviting and challenging them to become his disciples.* For this reason, catechesis is an essential component of youth ministry and one that needs renewed emphasis. If we are to succeed, we must offer young people a *spiritually challenging* and *world-shaping vision* that meets their hunger for the chance to *participate in a worthy adventure.* In the words of the Holy Father:

> This is what is needed: a Church for young people, which will know how to speak to their heart and enkindle, comfort, and inspire enthusiasm in it with the joy of the Gospel and the strength of the Eucharist; a Church which will know how to invite and to welcome the person who seeks a purpose for which to commit his whole existence; a Church which is not afraid to require much, after having given much; which does not fear asking from young people the effort of a noble and authentic adventure, such as that of the following of the Gospel (John Paul II, 1995 *World Day of Prayer for Vocations*).

We are confident that young people will commit themselves totally to Jesus Christ, who will ask everything from them and give everything in return. We need to provide concrete ways by which the demands, excitement, and adventure of being a disciple of Jesus Christ can be personally experienced by adolescents—where they tax and test their resources and where they stretch their present capacities and skills to the limits. Young people need to have a true opportunity for exploring what discipleship ultimately involves. This should include a partnership between youth ministers and the Diocesan Offices of Vocations and Family Life, offering young people an understanding of vocation that includes Christian marriage, generous single life, priesthood, religious life, diaconate, and lay ministry. Young people need to know and be known by the Church's ministers if they are to better understand how God is calling them to live as disciples. Faith-filled example by these ministers and active encouragement and invitations to consider a vocation to the priesthood and consecrated life will enable more to respond. Our young people will become truly convinced that "No one has greater love than this, to lay down one's life for one's friends" (Jn 15:13). Growth in discipleship is not about offering a particular program; it is the *goal* of all our efforts.

Goal 2: To draw young people to responsible participation in the life, mission, and work of the Catholic faith community.

Young people experience the Catholic community of faith at home, in the parish (especially in youth ministry programs), in Catholic schools, and in other organizations serving youth. Ministry with adolescents recognizes the importance of each of these faith communities in helping young people grow in faith as they experience life in community and actively participate in the mission of Jesus Christ and his Church.

The Family Community—the Church of the Home

In *Follow the Way of Love* we wrote, "A family is our first community and the most basic way in which the Lord gathers us, forms us, and acts in the world" (p. 8). We believe that family life is sacred because family relationships confirm and deepen family members' union with God and allow God's Spirit to work through them. The profound and ordinary moments of daily life are the threads from which families can weave a pattern of holiness. In *Follow the Way of Love*, we called families "to create a community of love, to help each other to grow, and to serve those in need" (ibid). We identified this work as a "participation in the work of the Lord, a sharing in the mission of the Church" (ibid). Adolescents need to experience the Catholic faith at home and participate in the Lord's mission with their families.

Adolescents enhance family life with their love and faith. The new understandings and skills they bring home from parish and school programs can enrich family life. Their growth in faith and active participation in parish life can encourage the entire family to make the Catholic faith central in their lives. The Church can contribute significantly toward strong, life-shaping families for young people by equipping, supporting, and encouraging families with adolescents to engage in family faith conversations; to teach moral values; to develop healthy relationships and use good communication skills; to celebrate family rituals; to pray together; to participate in shared service activities; to explore and discuss vocations to the priesthood and consecrated life; and to nurture close parental relationships and parental faith. One of the most important tasks for the Church today is to promote the faith growth of families by encouraging families to share, celebrate, and live their faith at home and in the world.

The Parish Community

The parish is where the Church lives. Parishes are communities of faith, of action, and of hope. They are where the Gospel is proclaimed and celebrated, where believers are formed and sent to renew the earth. Parishes are the home of the Christian community; they are the heart of our Church. Parishes are the place where God's people meet Jesus in word and sacrament and come in touch with the source of the Church's life (*Communities of Salt and Light*, p. 1).

The parish community has a special role in promoting participation in the life, mission, and work of the faith community.

First, parishes "should be a place where [young people] are welcomed, grow in Jesus Christ, and minister side by side with the adults of the community" (*A Message to Youth*). In parishes, young people should feel a sense of belonging and acceptance as full-fledged members of the community. Young people are more likely to gain a sense of identity in the community if they are regarded as full-fledged members.

Second, parishes "should have programs for [young people] that recognize [their] special talents and role in the life of the Church. [They] bring to the parish community youthfulness, energy, vitality, hopefulness, and vision" (ibid). In parishes, young people need to have a wide variety of opportunities to use their gifts and to express their faith through meaningful roles. They will develop a spirit of commitment within a community only through actual involvement in the many ways the Church exercises and carries out its mission. Especially crucial is the interaction with those who have made a lifetime commitment to serving the Church as priests, sisters, brothers, and deacons; young people need to know that such service is both rewarding and fulfilling.

Third, if parishes are to be worthy of the loyalty and active participation of youth, they will need to become "youth-friendly" communities in which youth have a conspicuous presence in parish life. These are parish communities that value young people—welcoming them into their midst; listening to them; responding to their needs; supporting them with prayer, time, facilities, and money. These are parish communities that see young people as resources—recognizing and empowering their gifts and talents, giving them meaningful roles in leadership and ministry, and encouraging their contributions. These are parish communities that provide young people with opportunities for intergenerational relationships—developing relationships with adults who serve as role models and mentors. In short, "youth-friendly" parish communities make a commitment to young people and their growth.

The Catholic School Community

As a faith community, Catholic schools provide young people with opportunities to deepen their understanding of the Catholic faith, to experience life in a Christian community, to participate actively in the mission of Jesus Christ and his Church, and to celebrate their Catholic faith. Catholic schools create a living faith community in which young people are empowered to utilize their gifts and talents and to live their faith through a variety of meaningful roles in the school, the parish, and in the Church at large. Catholic schools provide a unique opportunity for young people to experience the Gospel of Jesus Christ and to bring Catholic beliefs and values into their lives and the world. Campus ministry provides an essential element in the ministerial life of the Catholic school community and campus ministry fosters the faith development of young people and the entire school community through effective religious education and a variety of programs and activities, such as service projects, retreats, prayer services and liturgies, spiritual formation programs, leadership training, peer ministry, and vocation ministry that includes education, encouragement, and invitation.

In partnership with parents and parishes, Catholic schools prepare young people to become full and active members of the Catholic Church. Families, parishes, and Catholic schools continuously need to find ways to strengthen this partnership so that the lives of all young people are enriched and the resources of the Catholic community are wisely used. Some of these activities can be adapted for parish youth ministry.

The Youth-Serving Organizational Community

Catholic leaders in certain youth-serving organizations,[5] both within and outside of parishes, have a unique opportunity of reaching Catholic adolescents and bringing them into communion with the greater Catholic community. Through church-developed religious programs and activities, Catholic lay leaders and chaplains/moderators guide youth and act as mentors in their faith development, particularly in learning the gospel message and the basic teachings of the Church. These organizations are communities that help young people deepen their relationship with God and develop a spirit of joyful giving. These organizations afford an environment where adolescents can learn and can practice leadership skills and can focus on ethical decision making. Often, these organizations are able to reach at-risk youth and to provide much needed care and support. Wherever possible, it is important that these organizations provide adolescents the opportunity to participate in the life of their parish and diocese.

Goal 3: To foster the total personal and spiritual growth of each young person.

Ministry with adolescents promotes the growth of healthy, competent, caring, and faith-filled Catholic young people. The Church is concerned for the whole person, addressing the young people's spiritual needs in the context of his or her whole life. Ministry with adolescents fosters positive adolescent development *and* growth in both Christian discipleship and Catholic identity. Promoting the growth of young and older adolescents means addressing their unique developmental, social, and religious needs and nurturing the qualities or assets necessary for positive development. It also means addressing the *objective* obstacles to healthy growth that affect the lives of so many young people, such as poverty, racial discrimination, and social injustice, as well as the *subjective* obstacles to healthy growth such as the loss of a sense of sin, the influence of values promoted by the secular media, and the negative impact of the consumer mentality.

The Goals in Action

Research and pastoral experiences have demonstrated that there are particular assets—knowledge, values, skills, and commitments—that can make a significant difference in promoting the faith development of young and older adolescents. These assets focus our ministry by naming what the Church seeks to achieve in the lives of young people. They provide specific directions for effective pastoral practice that is guided by the three goals. These assets are nurtured in the home, in the Catholic school, in the parish community, and in the community at large through schools and organizations. We offer the following assets as a foundation for healthy faith development and growth in adolescents.[6] They are not intended as a final statement, but rather a solid guide to nurturing adolescent faith development and achieving the Church's goals.

The Church's ministry with adolescents seeks to

- guide young people in the call to holiness by developing a personal relationship with Jesus Christ by meeting him in the Scriptures, in the life and teachings of the Catholic Church, and in their own prayer lives;
- empower young people with the knowledge and skills for active participation in the life and ministries of the Church, including a comprehensive and substantive catechesis based on the catechism of the Catholic Church;
- nurture in young people positive, Catholic values of love, honesty, courage, peace and nonviolence, fidelity, chastity, generosity, tolerance, respect for life from conception to natural death, care and compassion, service to those in need, equality, social justice, integrity, responsibility, and community;
- help young people apply their Catholic faith to daily life experiences, nurture in young people a lifelong commitment to the Catholic faith, guiding them in developing a personal faith and skills for continuing their growth as Catholics;
- empower young people to live the moral and theological virtues and apply these virtues in making moral decisions;
- develop the biblical and doctrinal literacy of young people and a deeper appreciation for the importance of the Scriptures and the teachings of the Church in the Christian life;
- foster development of a personal spirituality and prayer life in young people;

- nurture in young people an understanding of and active participation in the sacramental life of the Church, especially the eucharist;
- help young people recognize that the Catholic faith calls them to work for justice and to defend human dignity;
- empower young people to serve those in need, to develop skills that foster social changes to secure justice and equality for every human being, and to live a life of Christian service modeled on Jesus' life;
- empower young people to become healers and reconcilers when conflicts arise, to pursue peace, and to become peaceful persons;
- promote an understanding of and respect for people who are different from the young people—different cultures, different languages, different faiths, different ages—and develop the attitudes and skills for overcoming racial and ethnic prejudices as individuals and members of society;
- develop young people's critical thinking skills that empower them to analyze contemporary life and culture in light of the Good News of Jesus Christ and the teachings of the Church;
- promote Catholic sexual values and attitudes and the importance of valuing chastity and sexual restraint;
- promote positive self-image in young people, including an appreciation of one's ethnic culture, a sense of self-esteem, a sense of purpose in life, a positive view of one's personal future, and a humble acceptance of one's self as lovable and loved by God and others;
- develop the life skills of adolescents including the skills for entering into and maintaining meaningful friendships, planning and decision-making skills, life-planning skills, appreciation and understanding of a variety of cultures, and peaceful conflict resolution skills;
- help young people recognize the movement of the Holy Spirit in their lives and discern their particular Christian vocation in the world—in the workplace, in marriage or single life, in the priesthood or conse-crated life, or in the permanent diaconate;
- cultivate the gifts and talents of young people, and empower them to utilize these gifts and talents in leadership and ministry in the

Church and community including peer ministry and intergenerational skills.

PART THREE

Themes and Components for a Comprehensive Ministry with Adolescents

Comprehensive Ministry with Adolescents—It Takes a Whole Church[7]

Since the 1970s, the Church has learned a great deal about ministry with adolescents. Through the hard work of countless leaders in parishes, schools, and dioceses across the United States, we have discovered effective approaches, strategies, programs, and activities. We also have learned that no one strategy, activity, or program is adequate to the task of promoting the three goals for ministry with adolescents and that families, parishes, and schools cannot work in isolation if the Church is to realize its goals. We have learned that it takes the entire Church to achieve the three goals we have established for ministry with adolescents.

Today, we propose a framework for integrating the Church's ministry with adolescents that incorporates a broader, expanded, and more comprehensive vision. First articulated in *A Vision of Youth Ministry* and developed more fully over the past two decades, the comprehensive approach is a framework for integration rather than a specific model. The comprehensive approach is not a single program or recipe for ministry. Rather, it provides a way for integrating ministry with adolescents and their families into the total life and mission of the Church, recognizing that the whole community is responsible for this ministry. The comprehensive approach uses *all* of our resources as a faith community—people, ministries, programs—in a common effort to promote the three goals of the Church's ministry with adolescents. The goals for ministry with adolescents help to keep our vision focused on the objectives. The themes provide a continuous thread that ensures that ministry with adolescents utilizes all available resources and is all-inclusive. The components highlight specific areas of ministry for a comprehensive approach. By offering this framework, we seek to provide direction to the Church's ministry *and* to affirm and encourage local creativity.

The comprehensive framework for ministry with adolescents is designed to

- utilize each of the Church's ministries—advocacy, catechesis, community life, evangelization, justice and service, leadership development, pastoral care, prayer and worship—in an integrated approach to achieving the three goals for ministry with adolescents;
- provide developmentally appropriate programs and activities that promote personal and spiritual growth for young and older adolescents;
- enrich family life and promote the faith growth of families of adolescents;
- incorporate young people fully into all aspects of church life and engage them in ministry and leadership in the faith community;
- create partnerships among families, schools, churches, and community organizations in a common effort to promote positive youth development.

Themes of a Comprehensive Vision

Developmentally Appropriate

Human development and growth in faith is a lifelong journey. *Renewing the Vision* builds upon the growth nurtured in childhood and provides a foundation for continuing growth in young adulthood. Effective ministry with adolescents provides developmentally appropriate experiences, programs, activities, strategies, resources, content, and processes to address the unique developmental and social needs of young and older adolescents both as individuals and as members of families. This approach responds to adolescents' unique needs, focuses ministry efforts, and establishes realistic expectations for growth during adolescence.

The assets proposed at the conclusion of Part Two are offered as a way to promote developmentally appropriate growth during adolescence.

Family Friendly

Ministry with adolescents recognizes that the family has the primary responsibility for the faith formation of young people and that the parish and Catholic school share in it. The home is a primary context for sharing, celebrating, and living the Catholic faith, and we are partners with parents in developing the faith life of their adolescent children. The Church can contribute significantly toward strong, life-shaping families for young people (see Goal Two). The changes in family life, such as the increasing diversity in family structure, the pressures of family time and commitments, and the changing economic situation, challenge us to respond to family needs and to develop a variety of approaches, programs, activities, and strategies to reach out to families.

The home is the Domestic Church, the "first and vital cell of society," the primary educators of faith and virtues. Since the family is the first place where ministry to adolescents usually occurs, the Church is at the service of parents to help them enliven within their children a knowledge and love for the Catholic faith.

The family has the mission to "guard, reveal, and communicate love." The family is the central place where the community of life and love are celebrated. Therefore, the Church's ministry with adolescents should lead young people into a deeper faith life within their own families. In other words, ministry with adolescents should not take adolescents away from the family, but rather foster family life.

Ministry with adolescents becomes family friendly by incorporating a family perspective into all parish and school policies, programs, and activities so that all ministry enriches family life in a way that affirms the sacramentality of Christian marriage and the mission of Christian marriage and the mission of the Catholic family in today's world and also is sensitive to the reality of families today. Ministry with adolescents also helps families at home, individually, and with other families by providing programs, activities, resources, and strategies designed to enrich and to promote family life and faith.

Intergenerational

Ministry with adolescents recognizes the importance of the intergenerational faith community in sharing faith and promoting healthy growth in adolescents. Meaningful involvement in parish life and the development of intergenerational relationships provide young people with rich resources to learn the story of the Catholic faith experientially and to develop a sense of belonging to the Church. Ministry with adolescents can incorporate young people into the intergenerational opportunities already available in the parish community, identify and develop leadership opportunities in the parish for young people, and create intergenerational support networks and mentoring relationships. Age-specific programs can be transformed into intergenerational programming and new intergenerational programs that incorporate young people can be developed.

Multicultural

Adolescents today are growing up in a culturally diverse society. The perceived image of the United States has shifted from a melting pot to a multihued tapestry. The strength and beauty of the tapestry lie in the diverse colors and textures of its component threads—the values and traditions claimed by the different racial and ethnic groups that constitute the people of the United States. Ministry with adolescents is multicultural when it focuses on a specialized ministry to youth of particular racial and ethnic cultures *and* promotes multicultural awareness among all youth.

First, ministry with adolescents recognizes, values, and responds to the diverse ethnic and cultural backgrounds and experiences that exist among adolescents·and develops culturally responsive and inclusive programming to address these needs. A fully multicultural approach to positive adolescent development and faith growth views ethnicity and culture as core features of identity and behavior. It helps youth identify and explore their own ethnic roots and cultural expressions in order to understand their own and others' ethnic practices. It recognizes that the specific content of adolescent tasks and competencies varies by culture, such as the way young people attain individual autonomy. It also recognizes the impact that family ethnicity has on adolescent development in areas such as decision making and social relationships. Ministry with adolescents helps young people develop their identity by affirming and utilizing the values and traditions of their ethnic cultures. Specifically, it welcomes and empowers *all* young people; it develops leaders who reflect the ethnic characteristics of the programs' participants; it trains all staff to be competent culturally; it includes young people and their families on advisory councils; and it develops program content that is culturally appropriate and relevant to the needs of participants. In stressing with our young Catholics the importance of multicultural awareness, and awareness of difference and diversity, we should take care to balance this awareness with the concept of their belonging to a universal Church, that is, with the concept of *unity* in diversity that characterizes the universal Church.

Second, *all* ministry with adolescents needs to incorporate ethnic traditions, values, and rituals into ministerial programming; teach about the variety of ethnic cultures in the Catholic Church; provide opportunities for crosscultural experiences; and foster acceptance and respect for cultural diversity. This approach helps young people learn about, understand, and appreciate people with backgrounds different from their own. Ministry with adolescents needs to counteract prejudice, racism, and discrimination by example, with youth themselves becoming models of fairness and nondiscrimination. In addition, programs in racism and oppression awareness are needed to foster effective communication skills in a multicultural context and to help young people develop skills for dealing with and overcoming social barriers to achievement.

Community-wide Collaboration

The Church's concern for the civic community includes advocacy on behalf of young people when public issues that affect their lives need to be addressed. Ministry with adolescents involves creating healthier civic communities for all young people. This involves networking with leaders in congregations of diverse faith traditions, public schools, youth-serving agencies, and community organizations to nurture a shared commitment to promoting healthy adolescent development and a healthy community; to develop mutual respect and understanding; to share resources; and to plan community-wide efforts and programs. Building these relationships can open doors for sharing resources and co-sponsoring training, programs, and advocacy efforts. Community-wide efforts are needed to serve the marginalized young people who lack the support and nurture of congregations and community and who are often the most vulnerable in our community. Community collaboration means building partnerships among families, schools, churches, and organizations that mobilize the community in a common effort to build a healthier community life and to promote positive adolescent development.

Leadership

Ministry with adolescents mobilizes *all* of the resources of the faith community in a comprehensive and integrated approach: "Part of the vision of youth ministry is to present to youth the richness of the person of Christ, which perhaps exceeds the ability of one person to capture, but which might be effected by the collective ministry of the many persons who make up the Church" (*A Vision of Youth Ministry*, p. 24). This approach involves a wide diversity of adult *and* youth leaders in a variety of roles necessary for comprehensive ministry. Ministry coordinators have a central role in facilitating the people, programming, and resources of the faith community on behalf of a comprehensive ministry effort with adolescents. Coordination is stewardship—overseeing the resources of the community so that they are used wisely in ministry with adolescents. Ministry coordinators alert the whole community to its responsibility for young people, draw forth the community's gifts and resources, and encourage and empower the community to minister with young people. Of special importance to effective ministry with adolescents is cooperation among the leaders, ministries, and programs in a faith community as they work together in a common effort to achieve the three goals of the Church's ministry with youth.

Flexible and Adaptable Programming

Ministry with adolescents creates flexible and adaptable program structures that address the changing needs and life situations of today's young people and their families within a particular community. The comprehensive approach incorporates the following elements in developing ministry programming for adolescents:

- a diversity of program settings
- age-specific programs for young and older adolescents
- family-centered programs for the entire family, for parents, for foster parents, for grandparents raising children, adolescents
- intergenerational parish programs
- community-wide programs
- a balanced mix of programs, activities, and strategies that address the eight components of comprehensive ministry described in the next section
- a variety of approaches to reach *all* adolescents and their families, including parish, school, and community-wide programs
- small-group programs and small ecclesial community experiences
- home-based programs, activities, and resources
- one-on-one and mentoring programs and activities
- independent or self-directed programs
- a variety of scheduling options and program settings to respond to the reality of the busy lives and commitments of adolescents and their families
- use of current technology to facilitate communication in program development and implementation

Components of a Comprehensive Ministry

Ministry with adolescents utilizes each of the Church's ministries—advocacy, catechesis, community life, evangelization, justice and service, leadership development, pastoral care, prayer and worship—in an integrated approach to achieve the three goals for ministry, discussed in Part Two.[8] First articulated in *A Vision of Youth Ministry*, these ministry components describe the "essence" of ministry with adolescents and provide the Church with eight fundamental ways to minister effectively with adolescents. Today, in light of our National Strategy on Vocations, we add vocational discernment to the "essence" of ministry with adolescents. These components provide a framework for the Catholic community to *respond* to the needs of young people and to *involve* young people in sharing their unique gifts with the larger community. They provide a structure for the Church's ministry with adolescents, while encouraging local creativity in developing programs, activities, and strategies for each component. Each ministry component supports and enhances the others. A comprehensive ministry with adolescents provides balance among all eight components. This balance can be achieved throughout a year or a season of programming. Even a single program or strategy can incorporate several of the ministry components, as in the case of a retreat program.[9]

The Ministry of Advocacy

Open your mouth in behalf of the [mute], and for the rights of the destitute; Open your mouth, decree what is just, defend the needy and the poor (Prv 31:8–9).

We seek to shape a society—and a world—with a clear priority for families and children [adolescents] in need and to contribute to the development of policies that help families protect their children's lives and overcome the moral, social, and economic forces that threaten their future. . . . As believers and citizens, we need—each of us—to use our values, voices, and votes to hold our public officials accountable and to shape a society that puts our children first (*Putting Children and Families First*, pp. 1, 7).

The ministry of advocacy engages the Church to examine its priorities and practices to determine how well young people are integrated into the life, mission, and work of the Catholic community. It places adolescents and families first by analyzing every policy and program—domestic, parish-based, diocesan, and international—for its impact on adolescents and families. Poor, vulnerable, and at-risk adolescents have first claim on our common efforts. The ministry of advocacy struggles against economic and social forces that threaten adolescents and family life, such as poverty, unemployment, lack of access to affordable health care, lack of decent housing, and discrimination. The ministry of advocacy supports policies and programs that support and empower adolescents and their families and works to overcome poverty, provide decent jobs, and promote equal opportunity. In all advocacy efforts we must remember to focus on adolescents and families with the greatest need. This is the "option for the poor" in action (*Putting Children and Families First*).

As a Church, we need to provide strong moral leadership; to stand up for adolescents, especially those who are voiceless and powerless in society. We call upon all ministry leaders and faith communities to use the resources of our faith community, the resources and talents of all our people, and the opportunities of this democracy to shape a society more respectful of the life, dignity, and rights of adolescents and their families.

The ministry of advocacy includes
- affirming and protecting the sanctity of human life as a gift from God and building societal respect for those who most need protection and support— the unborn, the poor, the disadvantaged, the sick, and the elderly;
- standing with and speaking on behalf of young people and their families on public issues that affect their lives, such as support for education,

quality housing, employment opportunities, access to health care, safe neighborhoods, and availability of meaningful community activities and services (We can help lift up the moral and human dimensions of public issues, calling the faith community to informed participation in the political process. We need to find ways to influence the political arena without being partisan: joining legislative networks, community organizations, and other advocacy groups. In election years, we can sponsor educational programs and forums to involve and inform others. Adolescents cannot be heard in the clamor of political and community debate and thus need strong champions for their interests.);

- empowering young people by giving them a voice and calling them to responsibility and accountability around the issues that affect them and their future (This involves education, leadership training, skills building, and organization to mobilize young people for action.);

- developing partnerships and initiatives with leaders and concerned citizens from all sectors of the community to develop a shared vision and practical strategies for building a healthy community. These partnerships also create opportunities for community-wide initiatives to address critical issues affecting adolescents and their families.

The ministry of advocacy encourages the Church to examine its practice of fully integrating adolescents into the life of the Church. How are the voices of young people honored and heard in the Church? How are the gifts, talents, and energy of young people respected and utilized within our faith communities? It is imperative that the Church models what it advocates for society.

The Ministry of Catechesis

Quite early on, the name catechesis was given to the totality of the Church's efforts to make disciples, to help people believe that Jesus is the Son of God so that believing they might have life in his name, and to educate and instruct them in this life, thus building up the Body of Christ (*Catechism of the Catholic Church* no. 4).

The ministry of catechesis helps adolescents *develop* a deeper relationship with Jesus Christ and the Christian community, and *increase* their knowledge of the core content of the Catholic faith. The ministry of Catechesis also helps young people *enrich* and *expand* their understanding of the Scriptures and the sacred tradition and their application to life today, and *live* more faithfully as disciples of Jesus Christ in their daily lives, especially through a life of prayer, justice, and loving service. Genuine faith is a total response of the whole person—mind, heart, and will. The ministry of catechesis fosters growth in Catholic faith in all three dimensions—trusting (heart), knowing and believing (mind), and doing (will). The goal should be to have all Catholic youth involved in some program of catechesis.

The ministry of catechesis with adolescents has several distinct features that give direction to catechetical programming. Specifically, catechesis with adolescents

- recognizes that faith development is lifelong and therefore provides developmentally appropriate content and processes around key themes of the Catholic faith that are responsive to the age-appropriate needs, interests, and concerns of young and older adolescents;
- teaches the core content of the Catholic faith as presented in the *Catechism of the Catholic Church*—the profession of faith, celebration of the Christian mystery, life in Christ, and Christian prayer—in order to provide a solid foundation for continued growth in faith;
- integrates knowledge of the Catholic faith with the development of practical skills for living the Catholic faith in today's world;
- utilizes the life experience of adolescents, fostering a shared dialogue between the life of the adolescent—with its joys, struggles, questions, concerns, and hopes—and the wisdom of the Catholic faith;
- engages adolescents in the learning process by incorporating a variety of learning methods and activities through which adolescents can explore and learn important religious concepts of the Scriptures and Catholic faith. A variety of learning approaches keeps interest alive among adolescents and responds to their different learning styles;

- involves group participation in an environment that is characterized by warmth, trust, acceptance, and care, so that young people can hear and respond to God's call (This fosters the freedom to search and question, to express one's own point of view, and to respond in faith to that call.);
- provides for real-life application of learning by helping adolescents apply their learning to living more faithfully as Catholic adolescents— considering the next steps that they will take and the obstacles that they will face;
- promotes family faith development through parish and school programs by providing parent education programs and resources, by incorporating a family perspective in catechetical programming, and by providing parent-adolescent and intergenerational catechetical programming;
- recognizes and celebrates multicultural diversity by including stories, songs, dances, feasts, values, rituals, saints, and heroes from the rich heritage of various cultures;
- incorporates a variety of program approaches including parish and school programs; small-group programs; home-based programs, activities, and resources; one-on-one and mentoring programs; and independent or self-directed programs or activities;
- explicitly invites young people to explore the possibility of a personal call to ministry and the beauty of the total gift of self for the sake of the kingdom.

The ministry of catechesis most effectively promotes the faith development of young and older adolescents when the curriculum is focused on important faith themes drawn from the teachings of the Church *and* on the developmental needs and life experiences of adolescents. The following faith themes have demonstrated their significance within the context of lifelong faith development and learning. Their selection is designed to "shed the light of the Christian message on the realities which have great impact on the adolescent" (GCD 84). This framework, organized around the four pillars of the *Catechism of the Catholic Church*, is offered as the basis of developing a catechetical curriculum for younger and older adolescents. Additional faith themes may need to be included to address local needs.[10]

Faith Themes for Young Adolescents
THE PROFESSION OF FAITH
- *Catholic Beliefs*—understanding the Creed and the core beliefs of the Catholic faith.
- *Holy Trinity*—introduction to God's unique self-revelation as three in one and some implications for living Christian faith and spiritual life.
- *Jesus Christ*—exploring the meaning of the Incarnation, the life and teachings of Jesus Christ, his death and resurrection, and the call to discipleship.
- *Church*—understanding the origins of the Church in Jesus Christ and understanding and experiencing the history of the Church and its mission.

THE SACRAMENTS OF FAITH
- *Sacraments*—understanding the role of the sacraments in the Christian life and experiencing the Church's celebration of the sacraments.
- *The Church*—understanding the reason for and beauty of the Church; identifying the necessity of the Church for our salvation.
- *Church Year*—understanding the meaning of the liturgical seasons of the Church year and the scriptural teachings presented through the Lectionary.

THE LIFE OF FAITH
- *Life in the Spirit*—understanding how the Spirit dwells in our midst in a new way since Pentecost and understanding that God's love has been poured into our hearts through the Holy Spirit who has been given to us.
- *The Dignity of the Human Person*—recognizing the divine image present in every human person.
- *Morality and Living a Virtuous Life*—incorporating Catholic moral

principles and virtues into one's life and moral decision making.

- *Personal Growth*—discerning the Spirit at work in their lives and incorporating the Catholic vision of life into personal identity.
- *Relationships*—developing and maintaining relationships based on Catholic values and the meaning of Christian community.
- *Sexuality*—understanding the Church's teaching on sexual morality, understanding the Church's positive view of sexuality as a gift from God, and understanding the importance of valuing chastity and sexual restraint.
- *Social Justice and Service*—understanding the importance of respecting the rights and responsibilities of the human person, appreciating our call to be stewards of creation, and discovering and living Jesus' call to a life of loving service.
- *Grace as Gift*—recognizing God's indwelling spirit in our lives and responding to this gift, which justifies and sanctifies us through God's law.
- *Lifestyles and Vocation*—discerning how to live the Christian vocation in the world, in the workplace, and in marriage, single life, ministerial priesthood, permanent diaconate, or consecrated life.

PRAYER IN THE LIFE OF FAITH

- *Christian Prayer*—understanding and experiencing the many forms of prayer in the Church—especially prayer through the church year—and the importance of the "Our Father" in Christian prayer.

Faith Themes for Older Adolescents
THE PROFESSION OF FAITH

- *Jesus Christ*—discovering the meaning of the life, death, and resurrection of Jesus and what this means for living in Christ's spirit today.
- *The Mystery of the Trinity*—understanding and experiencing the triune God.
- *Revelation*—understanding the revelation of sacred Scripture and sacred tradition.

- *Old Testament*—developing the knowledge and tools to read the Old Testament and to understand its meaning and challenge for us today.
- *The Gospels*—developing the knowledge and tools to read the Gospels and understand their meaning and challenge for us today.
- *Paul and His Letters*—developing the knowledge and tools to read Paul's letters and to understand their meaning and challenge for us today.
- *Faith and Identity*—exploring Catholic beliefs and what it means to live as a Catholic today.

The Sacraments of Faith

- *Sacraments of Initiation, Healing, and at the Service of Communion*—understanding the sacraments and how they are both personal and ecclesial, evoking a response from each of us.
- *Worship*—developing an understanding and skills for participating in the sacramental life of the Church, especially the eucharist.

The Life of Faith

- *Catholic Morality*—applying Catholic moral teachings to contemporary life situations as one encounters the many complexities in our world.
- *Conscience, Virtue, and Sin*—understanding and uncovering the desire to turn toward God and to do good and to act in accordance with God's grace, understanding the meaning and impact of sin, and learning to make decisions in accordance with one's rightly formed conscience.
- *Justice and Peace*—understanding that the Catholic faith calls people to work for justice, to pursue peace, and to defend human dignity, and developing skills to act for justice, peace, and human dignity.
- *Lifestyles and Vocation*—discerning how to live the Christian vocation in the world, in the workplace, and in marriage, single life, ministerial priesthood, permanent diaconate, or consecrated life.

PRAYER IN THE LIFE OF FAITH

- *Christian Prayer*—understanding and experiencing the variety of Christian prayer traditions and discovering and responding to the Spirit's personal invitation to develop a personal prayer life.

The Ministry of Community Life

> . . . You are a "chosen race, a royal priesthood, a holy nation, a people of his own . . ." (1Pt 2:9).

> The Church is the Body of Christ. Through the Spirit and his action in the sacraments, above all the Eucharist, Christ, who once was dead and is now risen, establishes the community of believers as his own Body. In the unity of this Body there is a diversity of members and functions. All members are linked to one another, especially to those who are suffering, to the poor and persecuted (*Catechism of the Catholic Church* nos. 805-806).

The ministry of community life *builds* an environment of love, support, appreciation for diversity, and judicious acceptance that models Catholic principles; *develops* meaningful relationships; and *nurtures* Catholic faith. The content of our message will be heard only when it is lived in our relationships and community life. To teach compassion, generosity, tolerance, peace, forgiveness, acceptance, and love as gospel values and to identify ourselves as Christians require us to live these values in our interactions with young people and in our community life. God's reign was proclaimed through the relationships Jesus initiated, and it continues to be heralded every time we witness our belief in him through the relationships in our community. The community life of the first Christians was a sign to everyone that Christ was in their midst (see Acts 2:42–47). The ministry of community life is not only *what* we do (activity), but *who* we are (identity) and *how* we interact (relationships).

Community life is nurtured when the *atmosphere* is welcoming, comfortable, safe, and predictable—one in which *all* adolescents know that their presence is welcomed, their energy is appreciated, and their contributions are valued. Community life is enhanced when leaders promote and model an *attitude* that is authentic, positive, accepting, and understanding—assuring *all* young people that they are valued and cared for as gifted individuals. Community life is encouraged when our *actions* are inviting, supportive, and gospel-based. Community life is created when *activities* build trust and encourage relationships, and are age-appropriate.

The ministry of community life with adolescents has several distinct features that give direction to community life programming. Specifically, community building with adolescents

- creates an environment characterized by gospel values that nurtures meaningful relationships among young people and between adolescents and adults;
- develops the friendship-making and friendship-maintaining skills of young people grounded in Christian values;
- enriches family relationships through programs, activities, and resources to improve skills such as family communication, decision making, and faith sharing;
- provides opportunities for multicultural community building that promote respect for young people's racial and ethnic cultures and develop skills for communication and understanding;
- engages adolescents in the life, activities, and ministries of the parish in meaningful and age-appropriate ways;
- provides avenues for adolescents to participate as members of the faith community and opportunities for the faith community to acknowledge, celebrate, and value its adolescent members;
- guides adolescents in developing
  — a healthy perspective of the joys and pains of relationships
  — skills that promote positive and healthy interaction

— an attitude of welcoming and acceptance

— an understanding of Jesus' call to "love your neighbor as yourself"

— an appreciation for both the uniqueness of individuals and the support of a community united through faith

— an awareness of the importance of their role as members of the community.

The Ministry of Evangelization

. . . [E]vangelizing means bringing the Good News of Jesus into every human situation and seeking to convert individuals and society by the divine power of the Gospel itself. Its essence is the proclamation of salvation in Jesus Christ and the response of a person in faith, both being the work of the Spirit of God (*Go and Make Disciples*, p. 2).

The ministry of evangelization shares the good news of the reign of God and invites young people to hear about the Word Made Flesh. Drawing from Jesus' example, evangelization involves the community's pronouncement and living witness that the reign of God has become realized in and through Jesus. The starting point for the ministry of evangelization "is our recognition of the presence of God already in young people, their experiences, their families, and their culture. . . . Through the Incarnation of God in Jesus, Christians are convinced that God is present within and through all of creation, and, in a special way, within humanity. Evangelization, therefore, enables young people to uncover and name the experience of a God already active and present in their lives. This provides an openness to the gift of the Good News of Jesus Christ" (*Challenge of Catholic Youth Evangelization* 7-8).

Evangelization is the energizing core of all ministry with adolescents. All of the relationships, ministry components, and programs of comprehensive ministry with adolescents must proclaim the Good News. They must invite young people into a deeper relationship with the Lord Jesus and empower them to live as his disciples.

The ministry of evangelization incorporates several essential elements: *witness, outreach, proclamation, invitation, conversion,* and *discipleship.*[11] Evangelization with adolescents

- proclaims Jesus Christ and the Good News so that young people will come to see in Jesus and his message a response to their hungers and a way to live. Remember: "There is no true evangelization if the name, the teaching, the life, the promises, the Kingdom and the mystery of Jesus of Nazareth, the Son of God, are not proclaimed" (*Evangelii Nuntiandi*, no. 22);

- witnesses to our faith in Jesus Christ in all aspects of our lives— offering ourselves and our community of faith as living models of the Christian faith in practice (Young people need to see that we are authentic and that our faith in Jesus guides our lives.);

- reaches out to young people by meeting them in their various life situations, building relationships, providing healing care and concern, offering a genuine response to their hungers and needs, and inviting them into a relationship with Jesus and the Christian community;

- invites young people personally into the life and mission of the Catholic community so that they may experience the support, nurture, and care necessary to live as Christians;

- calls young people to grow in a personal relationship with Jesus Christ, to make his message their own, and to join us in the continuing process of conversion to which the Gospel calls us;

- challenges young people to follow Jesus in a life of discipleship— shaping their lives in the vision, values, and teachings of Jesus and living his mission in their daily lives through witness and service;

- calls young people to be evangelizers of other young people, their families, and the community.

The Ministry of Justice and Service

Our faith calls us to work for justice; to serve those in need; to pursue peace; and to defend the life, dignity, and rights of all our sisters and brothers. This is the call of Jesus, the urging of his spirit, the challenge of the prophets, and the living tradition of our Church.

Our efforts to feed the hungry, shelter the homeless, comfort the sorrowing, console the bereaved, welcome the stranger, and serve the poor and vulnerable must be accompanied by concrete efforts to address the causes of human suffering and injustice. We believe advocacy and action to carry out our principles and constructive dialogue about how best to do this both strengthen our Church and enrich our society. We are called to transform our hearts and our social structures, to renew the face of the earth (see *A Century of Social Teaching*).

The ministry of justice and service *nurtures* in young people a social consciousness and a commitment to a life of justice and service rooted in their faith in Jesus Christ, in the Scriptures, and in Catholic social teaching; *empowers* young people to work for justice by concrete efforts to address the causes of human suffering; and *infuses* the concepts of justice, peace, and human dignity into all ministry efforts.

The Church increasingly views itself as a people set aside for the sake of others—a community that stands in solidarity with the poor, that reaches out in service to those in need, and that struggles to create a world where each person is treated with dignity and respect. We are called as a Church to respond to people's present needs or crises, such as homelessness or hunger. We are also called to help change the policies, structures, and systems that perpetuate injustice through legislative advocacy, community organizing, and work with social change organizations. Direct service needs to be coupled with action for justice so that adolescents experience the benefits of working directly with those in need *and* learn to change the system that keeps people in need. Justice and service are central to who we are as God's people and to how we live our faith at home, in our communities, and in the world.

> The central message is simple: our faith is profoundly social. We cannot be called truly "Catholic" unless we hear and heed the Church's call to serve those in need and work for justice and peace.

We cannot call ourselves followers of Jesus unless we take up his mission of bringing "good news to the poor, liberty to captives, and new sight to the blind" (cf. Lk 4:18) (*Communities of Salt and Light*, p. 3).

The ministry of justice and service with adolescents has several distinct features that give direction to programming and action. Specifically, justice and service with adolescents

- engages young people in discovering the call to justice and service in the Scriptures, in the life of Jesus, and in Catholic social teaching;
- involves adolescents, their families, and parish communities in actions of direct service to those in need and in efforts to address the causes of injustice and inequity;
- develops the assets, skills, and faith of young people by promoting gospel values in their lifestyles and choices; by increasing positive self-esteem, self-confidence, and moral reasoning abilities; by building leadership and social skills; by helping them discover their personal gifts and abilities; by helping them learn that they can make a difference in the world and receive recognition by the community for their contributions;
- incorporates doing the right thing with attention to why and how we do what we do (Four elements guide adolescents in moving from awareness to action on issues of justice. *Involvement* helps adolescents connect with justice issues personally and experientially. *Exploration* helps adolescents understand the causes, connections, and consequences of justice issues—expanding their knowledge and moving them toward action with a stronger background and motivation to work for real change when faced with injustice. *Reflection* helps adolescents utilize the Scriptures, Catholic social teachings, and the lived faith of the church community to discern a faith response to justice issues. *Action* helps adolescents respond to injustice through direct service or actions of social change—locally or globally, short term or long term.[12]);

- involves a supportive community that builds a sense of togetherness, nurtures a life of justice and service, works together to serve and act for justice, and provides support and affirmation;
- nurtures a lifelong commitment to service and justice involvement (This includes providing opportunities, support, and follow-up to help the young people reflect on their experience. People who learn to serve when they are young are more likely to be service oriented throughout their lives.).

The Ministry of Leadership Development

There are different kinds of spiritual gifts but the same Spirit; there are different forms of service but the same Lord; there are different workings by the same God who produces all of them in everyone. To each individual the manifestation of the Spirit is given for some benefit (1 Cor 12:4–7).

The ministry of Leadership Development *calls forth*, *affirms*, and *empowers* the diverse gifts, talents, and abilities of adults and young people in our faith communities for comprehensive ministry with adolescents. Leadership roles in adolescent ministry are key. Leaders must be trained and encouraged. This approach involves a wide diversity of adult *and* youth leaders in a variety of roles. Many will be involved in direct ministry with adolescents; others will provide support services and yet others will link the ministry effort to the resources of the broader community.

The ministry of leadership development has several important elements that provide direction. Specifically, leadership development

- utilizes adult and adolescent leaders in a variety of leadership roles necessary for comprehensive ministry (These roles include, but are not limited to, ministry coordinators in parishes and schools, school teachers, ministry program leaders and planning teams, overall ministry coordinating team, and support staff.):

— *The Ministry Coordinator*, must always be qualified and well trained, as well as have an excellent reputation. He or she facilitates the people, programming, and resources of the parish or school community in a comprehensive ministry effort. The coordinator is primarily responsible for facilitating planning, administering programs, developing a leadership system for adult and youth leaders (recruitment, training, and support), and serving as an advocate and link for young people to the faith community and wider community.

— *A Coordinating Team*, made up of adults and young people, may be formed to work with the ministry coordinator in organizing a comprehensive ministry with adolescents by planning the overall ministry, developing a leadership system, identifying the resources of the faith community, and connecting the ministry with the other ministries and programs of the faith community.

— *Program Leaders*—adults and adolescents—conduct specific programs and activities within a comprehensive ministry. Program leaders often work with a program planning team who develops, promotes, implements, and evaluates the program.

— *Support Staff* provide assistance that helps individual programs and the overall ministry function effectively.

• develops a leadership system that invites, trains, supports, and nourishes adult and adolescent leaders and provides for the coordination of leaders throughout a comprehensive ministry;

• develops and nurtures adult leaders of lively faith and maturity with solid theological understandings, relational and ministry skills, and organizational ability appropriate to their particular role in ministry with adolescents;

• empowers all young people for leadership and ministry with their peers—in schools, parishes, and civic communities—by affirming their gifts, equipping them with skills for leadership and ministry, and by placing them in leadership roles or giving them leadership opportunities where they can make a contribution.

We strongly encourage all ministry leaders and communities to call forth the gifts of all young people and empower them for ministry to their peers and leadership in our faith communities. We need their gifts, energy, and vitality. We echo the words of the Holy Father at World Youth Day in Denver:

> Young pilgrims, Christ needs you to enlighten the world and to show it the "path to life" (Ps 16). . . . Place your intelligence, your talents, your enthusiasm, your compassion, and your fortitude at the service of life. . . . The Church needs your energies, your enthusiasm, your youthful ideals, in order to make the Gospel of life penetrate the fabric of society, transforming people's hearts and the structures of society in order to create a civilization of true justice and love (August 15, 1993).

The Ministry of Pastoral Care

The ministry of pastoral care is a compassionate presence in imitation of Jesus' care of people, especially those who were hurting and in need. The ministry of Pastoral Care involves *promoting* positive adolescent and family development through a variety of positive (preventive) strategies; *caring* for adolescents and families in crisis through support, counseling, and referral to appropriate community agencies; *providing guidance* as young people face life decisions and make moral choices; and *challenging* systems that are obstacles to positive development (*advocacy*). Pastoral care is most fundamentally a relationship—a ministry of compassionate presence. This was Jesus' caring stance toward all people, especially those who were hurting or in need. Pastoral care enables healing and growth to take place within individuals and their relationships. It nurtures growth toward wholeness, and it provides guidance in decision making and challenges obstacles to positive development.

The ministry of pastoral care with adolescents has several distinct features that provide direction to comprehensive ministry efforts.

Specifically, pastoral care

- develops the life skills of adolescents, such as relationship building, assertivenesss, nonviolent conflict resolution, decision making, and planning;
- guides young people in making important life decisions, such as career and college choices, and discerning their particular Christian vocation;
- fosters the spiritual development of young people and the healthy integration of their sexuality and spirituality;
- creates networks of care and support for young people and their families;
- provides programs and resources for parent education and skills for effective parenting that incorporate understandings of adolescent development and family life cycle tasks;
- strengthens family life by assisting families to improve family skills, such as communication, decision making, problem solving, and reconciliation;
- provides and connects adolescents and families to support services, referral resources, and self-help groups to promote healing during times of loss, sudden change, unexpected crises, problems, and family or personal transitions;
- provides support and enrichment for adolescents and parents experiencing divorce, separation, or family problems; and connects them to appropriate counseling resources;
- collaborates with the wider community in providing direct aid to youth-at-risk in the form of programs, services, and counseling.

Special attention should be given to young people who engage in high-risk behaviors that endanger their own health and well-being. These young people often have multiple problems that can severely limit their futures—fragmented family life, poor school performance, antisocial behavior, eating disorders, sexual activity, sexual confusion as they struggle with identity, and alcohol or drug use, to name several. The Church is called to work with the wider community to address the needs of these young people. Ministry to these young people may be the most

important way they will ever come to know and feel the love of God—
through people who love them and care for them just at the point when
they themselves feel least worthy and lovable.

The Ministry of Prayer and Worship

"Great is the mystery of faith!" The Church professes this mystery
in the Apostles' Creed (*Part One*) and celebrates it in the sacramental liturgy (*Part Two*), so that the life of the faithful may be
conformed to Christ in the Holy Spirit to the glory of God the
Father (*Part Three*). This mystery, then, requires that the faithful
believe in it, that they celebrate it, and that they live from it in a
vital and personal relationship with the living and true God. This
relationship is prayer (*Catechism of the Catholic Church* no. 2558).

The ministry of prayer and worship *celebrates* and *deepens* young
people's relationship with Jesus Christ through the bestowal of grace,
communal prayer and liturgical experiences; it *awakens* their awareness
of the spirit at work in their lives; it *incorporates* young people more fully
into the sacramental life of the Church, especially eucharist; it *nurtures*
the personal prayer life of young people; and it *fosters* family rituals and
prayer.

The ministry of prayer and worship with adolescents has several distinct
dimensions that provide direction to comprehensive ministry efforts.[13]
Specifically, the ministry of prayer and worship

- promotes the authentic participation of youth in liturgy (Parishes and
  schools can acknowledge adolescent faith issues at all liturgies in ways
  appropriate to the rites, provide opportunities for young people to be
  trained as liturgical ministers, schedule periodic youth event liturgies
  that are prepared with young people's input and assistance, and invite
  young people to help prepare the community liturgies.);
- attends to the diversity of cultures and ages in the assembly (All liturgy
  takes place within a cultural milieu and context. Respect for cultures

and inclusion of native art, music, and expressions are visible components of vibrant worship. The rites need to reflect cultural diversity through the use of symbols, traditions, musical styles, and native language. Parishes and schools can provide opportunities for liturgical celebrations in which young people of different ethnic groups express their faith in their own language, symbols, and tradition. Parishes and schools can also provide experiences of other cultural worship styles and multicultural liturgies that bring people from all ethnic backgrounds together to celebrate. Adolescents reflect a distinct age group and "culture" within our society. Their language expressions, musical styles, and ways of life are often quite different from those of older generations. Those who prepare the liturgy need to find appropriate ways to incorporate the world of young people into worship, remembering that the "pastoral effectiveness of a celebration will be heightened if the texts of the readings, prayers, and songs correspond as closely as possible to the needs, religious dispositions, and aptitude of the participants" (GIRM no. 313). Parishes and schools can explore new music and song texts being composed for liturgy, and invite youth to act as cultural resources—letting the individuals or group know about current trends and expressions that may be reflected in the prayers, songs or rituals.);

- provides opportunities for creative prayer with adolescents in peer, family, and intergenerational settings (Ministry with adolescents fosters and promotes the development of a personal prayer life in young people and celebrates the ritual moments of their daily lives in prayer. The symbols and rituals of liturgy become more meaningful for young people when they draw from their experiences of private prayer. Likewise, private prayer is revitalized by meaningful experiences of the liturgy. Ministry with adolescents also promotes opportunities for communal prayer. The liturgy of the hours, liturgies of reconciliation and healing, ethnic rituals and celebrations, and other ritual devotions allow for creativity and adaptation to the life issues and cultural expressions of young people. Communal prayer provides opportunities for young people of different ethnic cultures to express their faith in their own language, symbols, and traditions and for young people to experience multicultural prayer that brings people from all racial and ethnic backgrounds together to celebrate. Parishes and schools can schedule seasonal prayer experiences for and by youth for the parish community, involve young people in the preparation of prayer experiences for their peers, provide prayer resources, include personal prayer time within programs, and provide prayer mentors for young people. Parishes and schools can provide prayer and ritual resources for home settings that address the unique needs of families with adolescents, the calendar and church year celebrations and rituals, and family rituals, rites of passages and milestones.);

- promotes effective preaching of the word (Parishes and schools can invite young people to reflect on the seasonal readings and to offer suggestions to the homilist for connections to young peoples' lives, provide regular opportunities for adolescents to study the Scriptures, encourage those who preach to use current examples and storytelling techniques, and investigate the developments within culture for their impact on the "vernacular.");

- allows music and song to express the vitality of young people (The music of the young brings freshness and variety to our current musical genres and can perform the same infusion of energy and vitality to sacred music. Music is a significant part of personal expression for young people and that desire carries over to their participation in liturgy. Parishes and schools can invite adolescents to participate in the choirs and musical assemblies, explore contemporary accompaniments and focus on the song and pace of the music, expand the local repertoire of hymns and songs to include songs that young people would select, and encourage singing by the whole assembly so that adolescents feel more comfortable in adding their voices.);

- prepares the symbols and ritual actions with particular care for their visual dimensions (Today's young people have been educated through multimedia. Their visual sense is one of their primary ways of learning and responding to the environment. Parishes and schools can invite adolescents to assess the visual dynamics of the rituals and symbols prepared for liturgy, provide visual aids to encourage young people's participation, and explore the appropriate use of multimedia at liturgy.);

- develops the interpersonal and communal dimensions of the liturgy. (Parishes and schools can focus on the hospitality provided at liturgy, encourage young people to attend liturgy with their friends, build a sense of community among young people prior to liturgy, minister in a personal way, and affirm the presence of young people whenever possible.);

- provides adolescents with effective and intentional catechesis for liturgy, worship, and sacraments (Young people are catechized by their participation in the liturgy; therefore, care must be taken to ensure that their experiences lead them to greater faith. Adolescents need catechesis for liturgy and the sacraments, but are also catechized by their experiences of liturgy. Through immersion in the symbols, stories, and rituals of the communal prayer life, adolescents gain not only a knowledge but an appreciation of the power of the sacraments. A specific objective of intentional catechesis for liturgy is to assist adolescents in exploring how liturgical symbols and rituals celebrate their experiences of God and life events. Parishes and schools can provide opportunities for intergenerational and family-centered catechesis for liturgy and can offer experiential, liturgical catechesis for young people.);

- apprentices adolescents in liturgical ministries (Ministry with adolescents can advocate for youth involvement in liturgical ministries and connect young people with established liturgical ministers for training and experience of actually performing liturgical ministry.).

PART FOUR

A Guiding Image for Ministry with Adolescents

> He summoned the Twelve and gave them power and authority
> over all demons and to cure diseases, and he sent them to proclaim
> the kingdom of God and to heal [the sick]. He said to them,
> "Take nothing for the journey, neither walking stick, nor sack,
> nor food, nor money, and let no one take a second tunic." . . .
> Then they set out and went from village to village proclaiming
> the good news and curing diseases everywhere (Lk 9:1–3, 6).

> How does Jesus send you? He promises neither sword, nor money,
> nor any of the things which the means of social communications
> make attractive to people today. He gives you instead grace and
> truth. He sends you out with the powerful message of his paschal
> mystery, with the truth of the cross and resurrection. That is all he
> gives you, and that is all you need (Pope John Paul II, World Youth
> Day 1996).

A Vision of Youth Ministry captured the dynamics of ministry with
adolescents through the story of the disciples on the road to Emmaus (see
Lk 24:13–35). This story became a guiding image for ministry with its
emphasis on the relationship between young disciples and their Lord, a
relationship characterized by presence, listening, faith sharing, and celebration. The Emmaus story will continue to guide the Church's ministry
with adolescents, but a new image is emerging—the image of young
people with a mission. Just as Jesus sent out the Twelve (Lk 9) and the
seventy-two (Lk 10) to carry out his mission, today he sends out young

people to proclaim the Good News and to build a world that is more just, more peaceful and more respectful of human life and creation. The Holy Father captured the urgency of young people's mission at World Youth Day 1993 in Denver.

> Young pilgrims, Christ needs you to enlighten the world and to show it the "path to life" (Ps 16:11). The challenge is to make the Church's yes to life concrete and effective. The struggle will be long, and it needs each one of you. Place your intelligence, your talents, your enthusiasm, your compassion, and your fortitude at the service of life.

> At this stage of history, the liberating message of the Gospel of life has been put into your hands. And the mission of proclaiming it to the ends of the earth is now passing to your generation. . . . The Church needs your energies, your enthusiasm, your youthful ideals, in order to make the Gospel of life penetrate the fabric of society, transforming people's hearts and the structures of society in order to create a civilization of true justice and love. Now more than ever, in a world that is often without light and without the courage of noble ideals, people need the fresh, vital spirituality of the Gospel.

> . . . The world at the approach of a new millennium . . . is like a field ready for the harvest. Christ needs laborers ready to work in his vineyards. May you, the Catholic young people of the world, not fail him. In your hands, carry the cross of Christ. On your lips, the words of life. In your hearts, the saving grace of the Lord (August 15, 1993).

The Church and world need the faith, gifts, energy, and fresh ideas of young people. The entire Church, and in a special way ministry with adolescents, must empower young people for their mission in the world. We must ensure that young people are well equipped for their special mission in the world. All of our efforts to promote an active Christian discipleship and growth in Catholic identity must lead toward mission. This is our special responsibility to the young generation. We pray with the whole Church that we can meet the challenge of *Gaudium et Spes*; ". . . the future of humanity lies in the hands of those who are strong enough to provide coming generations with reasons for living and hoping" (no. 31).

Notes

1. *New Directions in Youth Ministry: A New Study of Catholic Youth Ministry Program Participants* (Final Report, July 1996) conducted by the Center for Applied Research in the Apostolate (CARA) is available in full report or executive summary from the National Federation for Catholic Youth Ministry, 3700-A Oakview Terrace NE, Washington, DC 20017-2591. The following is a summary of the findings identified in the text.

Ways to Grow
When asked the areas in which youth ministry had most helped them to grow, young people named the following nine ways at the top of their list ("very much" responses):

- Understanding my Catholic faith better (52%)
- Making serious life choices (52%)
- Choosing right from wrong (50%)
- Having a safe and caring place to go (50%)
- Deepening my relationship with Jesus (49%)
- Experiencing what it means to be Catholic (48%)
- Discussing problems facing youth today (48%)
- Getting more involved in parish life (48%)
- Developing pride in who I am (48%)

Commitment to the Catholic Church
Almost all are "proud to be Catholic" (94%) and "admire the pope" (89%). Virtually all report that they "feel welcome at church" (90%). Females are more likely to support these statements than males.

Sunday Mass Attendance
Youth ministry program participants report more frequent attendance

at worship than their friends, their parents, or other adults significant in their lives. There is a strong connection between participation in youth ministry programs and Mass attendance.

- Fifty-eight percent attend Mass weekly and another 14 percent attend more than weekly, for a total of 72 percent who attend once a week or more.
- Another 12 percent report attendance on the order of once or twice a month.

Continued Growth

Youth ministry makes a deeper impression on participants the longer they participate. Perhaps the strongest way to measure the effectiveness of youth ministry is to contrast the ninth graders with the twelfth graders. For the thirty-five ways youth ministry could have helped, thirty-two were given much higher average scores by those in twelfth grade. Below are the eight areas with average scores that increased by twenty points or more when ninth graders are compared to twelfth graders.

- Developing my leadership skills (32 points)
- Developing my relationship skills (27 points)
- Discussing problems facing youth today (23 points)
- Preparing me to share my faith (22 points)
- Doing service projects to help other people (22 points)
- Feeling like I belong to a community (22 points)
- Providing ministry to my peers (22 points)
- Helping the Church better serve youth (20 points)

2. The Search Institute has identified several factors contributing to the breakdown:
   - Many adults no longer consider it their responsibility to play a role in the lives of youth outside their family.
   - Parents are less available for their children because of demands outside the home and cultural norms that undervalue parenting.

- Adults and institutions have become uncomfortable articulating values or enforcing appropriate boundaries for behavior.
- Society has become more and more age-segregated, providing fewer opportunities for meaningful intergenerational relationships.
- Socializing systems (families, schools, congregations, etc.) have become more isolated, competitive, and suspicious of each other.
- The mass media have become influential shapers of young people's attitudes, norms, and values.
- As problems—and solutions—have become more complex, more of the responsibility for young people has been turned over to professionals.

3. The forty developmental assets, identified through national research by the Search Institute, are powerful shapers of young people's behavior. Assets help to inoculate youth from high-risk behaviors (e.g., use of alcohol and drugs, antisocial behavior, sexual activity). As assets increase, the incidence of high-risk behaviors decreases. Developmental assets also promote positive outcomes. As assets increase, so do school success, the affirmation of diversity, educational aspirations, and prosocial behavior. Young people with a greater number of assets are more likely to grow up caring, competent, healthy, and responsible. This important relationship between developmental assets and choices made has been documented for all types of youth, regardless of age, gender, geographic region, town size, or race/ethnicity.

These forty developmental assets have been identified through research by the Search Institute (USA) as forming a foundation for healthy development in children and adolescents. The following information is excerpted from Search Institute research (© 1996 Search Institute).

External Assets

Support

Family Support—family life provides high levels of love and support.

Positive Family Communication—young person and her or his parent(s) communicate positively, and young person is willing to seek parental advice and counsel.

Other Adult Relationships—young person receives support from three or more nonparent adults.

Caring Neighborhood—young person experiences caring neighbors.

Caring School Climate—school provides a caring, encouraging environment.

Parent Involvement in Schooling—parent(s) are actively involved in helping young person succeed in school.

Empowerment

Community Values Youth—young person perceives that adults in the community value youth.

Youth as Resources—young people are given useful roles in the community.

Community Service—young person serves in the community one hour or more per week.

Safety—young person feels safe at home, at school, and in the neighborhood.

Boundaries and Expectations

Family Boundaries—family has clear rules and consequences, and monitors the young person's whereabouts.

School Boundaries—school provides clear rules and consequences.

Neighborhood Boundaries—neighbors take responsibility for monitoring young people's behavior.

Adult Role Models—parent(s) and other adults model positive, responsible behavior.

Positive Peer Influence—young person's best friends model responsible behavior.

High Expectations—both parent(s) and teachers encourage the young person to do well.

Time Use

Creative Activities—young person spends three or more hours per week in lessons or practice in music, theater, or other arts.

Youth Programs—young person spends three or more hours per week in sports, clubs, or organizations at school and/or in community organizations.

Religious Community—young person spends one or more hours per week in activities in a religious institution.

Time at Home—young person is out with friends "with nothing special to do" two or fewer nights per week.

Internal Assets

Educational Commitment

Achievement Motivation—young person is motivated to do well in school.

School Performance—young person has a B average or better.

Homework—young person reports doing at least one hour of homework every school day.

Bonding to School—young person cares about her or his school.

Reading for Pleasure—young person reads for pleasure three or more hours per week.

Positive Values

Caring—young person places high value on helping other people.

Equality and Social Justice—young person places high value on promoting equality and reducing hunger and poverty.

Integrity—young person acts on convictions and stands up for her or his beliefs.

Honesty—young person "tells the truth even when its not easy."

Responsibility—young person accepts and takes personal responsibility.

Restraint—young person believes it is important not to be sexually active or to use alcohol or other drugs.

Social Competencies

Planning and Decision Making—young person knows how to plan ahead and make choices.

Interpersonal Competence—young person has empathy, sensitivity, and friendship skills.

Cultural Competence—young person has knowledge or and comfort with people of different cultural/racial/ethnic backgrounds.

Resistance Skills—young person can resist negative peer pressure and dangerous situations.

Peaceful Conflict Resolution—young person seeks to resolve conflict nonviolently.

Positive Identity

Personal Power—young person feels he or she has control over "things that happen to me."

Self-Esteem—young person reports having a high self-esteem.

Sense of Purpose—young person reports that "my life has a purpose."

Positive View of Personal Future—young person is optimistic about her or his personal future.

4. Although these goals are numbered, they are considered to be equally important.

5. For example, scouting organizations, youth retreat movements, and organizations specifically serving at-risk youth.

6. These assets were developed from research by the Search Institute in Minneapolis and from Challenge of Adolescent Catechesis (NFCYM, 1986). These assets are intended as a guide, not as an evaluative tool.

7. Sr. Thea Bowman, FSPA, adapted the phrase "It Takes a Whole Church" from the Ghanian proverb "It takes a village to raise a child."

8. There is a variety of schemas for identifying the ministries of the Church. This document continues with the framework articulated in *A Vision of Youth Ministry*. While the names of the ministries may vary, the eight proposed in this paper reflect what the Church considers the basic pastoral work in a parish community as expressed in *The Code of Canon Law* (cf. Canons 528- 529):

   - ensuring that the word of God is proclaimed in its entirety to those living in the parish
   - instruction in the truths of faith, especially by means of the homily and by catechetical formation
   - works that promote the spirit of the Gospel, including its relevance to social justice
   - Catholic education of children and youth
   - bringing the gospel message to those who have given up religious practice or who do not profess the true faith (outreach to inactive Catholics)
   - promotion of eucharist as the center of the parish assembly
   - celebration of the sacraments, especially eucharist and penance (including programs of sacramental life and preparation)
   - nourishment of the prayer life of parishioners, especially within families
   - active participation of parishioners in the liturgy
   - methods of acquaintance with parishioners, the welcoming of newcomers, home visiting, efforts at building community
   - care for the sick and especially the dying

- concern and care for the poor, the suffering, the lonely, those who are exiled from their homeland, and those burdened with special difficulties
- foster the growth of Christian life in the family
- recognize and promote the specific role that the lay members of the parish have in the mission of the Church
- foster in parishioners concern and works that promote the community of the parish and that help them feel themselves to be members of the diocese and the universal Church.

9. The order of the components is alphabetical. No prioritizing of the eight components is intended by this order.

10. This list contains some of the faith themes found in *The Challenge of Adolescent Catechesis: Maturing in Faith* (Washington, D.C.: National Federation for Catholic Youth Ministry, 1986).

11. These elements are drawn from *The Challenge of Catholic Youth Evangelization: Called to Be Witnesses and Storytellers* (Washington, D.C.: National Federation for Catholic Youth Ministry, 1993).

12. This four-stage process is know as the Pastoral Circle and developed from the work of Peter Henriot and Joseph Holland.

13. The principles for worship and liturgy include many of the ideas found in the final draft of *From Age to Age: The Challenge of Worship with Adolescents* (Washington, D.C.: National Federation for Catholic Youth Ministry, 1997).